EXTREME
SCOOBY
The Ultimate
Scooby-Doo Trivia Book

EXTREME SCOOBY

The Ultimate Scooby-Doo Trivia Book

SCHOLASTIC INC.
New York Toronto London Auckland Sydney
Mexico City New Delhi Hong Kong

ISBN 0-590-63110-1

Designed by Lorraine Forte

Copyright © 1999 by Hanna-Barbera.

CARTOON NETWORK and logo are trademarks of
The Cartoon Network, Inc.

SCOOBY-DOO and all related characters and elements are trademarks
of Hanna-Barbera. All rights reserved. Published by Scholastic Inc.

SCHOLASTIC and associated logos are trademarks and/or
registered trademarks of Scholastic Inc.

12 11 10 9 8 7 6 5 4 3 2 1   9/9 0 1 2 3 4/0

Printed in the U.S.A.

First Scholastic printing, April 1999

Chapter 1   Scooby-Dooby-Doo—
Can You Dig This?   1

Chapter 2   Like, A Dude Named
Shaggy!   13

Chapter 3   Jinkies! The Vibe
on Velma!   22

Chapter 4   Fred Jones, Leader of
Mystery, Inc.   28

Chapter 5   Jeepers! It's Danger-
Prone Daphne   38

Chapter 6   Whoo-Hoo! Bring On
The Bad Guys!   42

Chapter 7   It's All Relative!   49

Chapter 8   The Gang's All Here   53

Chapter 9   All Scooby All The Time
The Episode Guide   61

HOW MUCH DOO YOU KNOW?

Like, wow! Scooby-Doo is everywhere — on Cartoon Network, on video, posters, T-shirts, lunch boxes, even underwear! That's because everyone, of every age, **LOVES** having Scooby around. He's the world's favorite ghoul-chasing, chickenhearted chowhound.

Zoinks! But just because everyone loves Scooby-Doo doesn't mean everyone's an expert. Are you?

Jinkies! Did you know that the very first episode of Scooby-Doo was about a black knight? Or that Velma's nickname for Shaggy and Scooby is "The Gulping Gourmets"?

Ruh-roh! Those snack bits, and tons more about super-sleuth Scooby and his friends, Shaggy, Velma, Fred, and Daphne, can be found in the pages of *Extreme Scooby: The Ultimate Scooby-Doo Trivia Book*.

So, just "Doo" it! If you want to be a Scooby expert, turn the page and say, "Scooby-Dooby-Doo!"

CHAPTER 1:
Scooby-Dooby-Doo!
Can You Dig This?

SCOOBER-IFIC SECRETS

- Rhythm 'n' Doo: Scooby is an *expert* dancer. He can also play the bugle, the ukulele, and the organ.

- Scooby's favorite part of a museum is where they keep the dinosaur bones. Yum!

- Scooby sleeps in a doghouse in Shaggy's backyard. Hope Shaggy doesn't snore too loud!

- Scooby is seven years old in human years. That's 49 in dog years. His show has been on since 1969! How old does *that* make Scooby in dog years?*

- Scooby is a master of disguise. He has masqueraded as Napoleon, a witch, a caveman, a knight in armor, a portrait painter, and even as one half of a cow!

* 30 x 7 = *210.*

- Scooby dislikes things that go bump in the night — like ghouls, goblins, ghosts, zombies, and monsters. In other words, he's just like everybody else!

- Our favorite hound has super-sensitive ears that can pick up the sound of danger from blocks away — although this is nothing compared to his super sniffer, which can smell food from *miles* away!

Tail-Wagging Trivia

When Scooby disguised himself as a fortune-teller, a customer asked for her palm to be *read*. Scooby painted it *red*!

BEHIND EVERY GOOD DOG IS A GOOD DOG'S BEHIND!

Tail-Wagging Trivia

Scooby once forced a villain out of hiding
by blocking a chimney with his "bottom."
The bad guy ran out coughing when the
room filled with smoke from the fireplace.
Scooby's a heroic canine —
no butts about it!

"TAILS" OF DERRING-DOO

Top five things Scooby can do with his tail:

- Open and close a door.
- Pick a lock.
- Twirl it like a lasso.
- Catch fish.
- Swing a huge hammer!

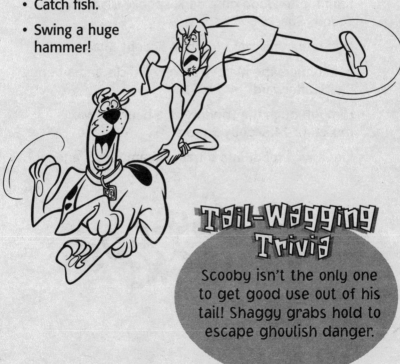

Tail-Wagging Trivia

Scooby isn't the only one to get good use out of his tail! Shaggy grabs hold to escape ghoulish danger.

"DOO"-ING THE MATH:
HOW MANY SCOOBY SNACKS
DOES IT TAKE FOR SCOOBY TO . . .

- act as decoy for a dognapper: 1 Scooby Snack
- get in an old, creaky elevator: 2 Scooby Snacks
- stand guard alone: 2 Scooby Snacks
- hunt for firewood on a dark, spooky island: 3 Scooby Snacks
- sniff out a graveyard tomb: 4 Scooby Snacks
- bait a huge Ape Man: 4 Scooby Snacks and a bonus Snack afterward
- climb through the window of a haunted wax museum: 24 Scooby Snacks
- lure a wild robot into a trap: No amount is enough!

SCOOBY SNACK FACT PACK: You can trick Scooby-Doo into a scary room by throwing in a Scooby Snack.

Scooby can locate Velma by following the scent of the Scooby Snacks she keeps with her.

WHAT IS SCOOBY-DOO'S REAL NAME?

A) Scooby-wan Kenobi

B) Scoobercalifragilisticexpialidocious

C) Scoobert

D) Scoop Doggie Dog

(See page 73 for the answer!)

Tail-Wagging Trivia

When he's camping out, Scooby always sleeps in a *pup* tent!

SCOOBY-DOO, MORE COOL FACTS ABOUT YOU!

- Wake-up call: Scooby can play reveille on his fingers like he's playing a bugle.

- Pool pooch: Scooby shoots a mean game of billiards.

- Tall tail: He's good at walking on stilts — if he can avoid the gopher holes!

- Hound dog: When it comes to the ladies, this gentleman dog prefers poodles.

- Super-scoob: Scoob's fingernail (or should that be pawnail?) can cut through wood.

- Scooby can fly like a bird if he grabs two trash-can lids and starts flapping his front legs. **CRASH!** He's not too good at landings, though!

- One of Scooby's favorite movies is *Star: Dog Ranger of the North Woods*.

- Scooby **LOVES** a good ear scratch. (But then, who doesn't?)

- "Doctor Scoolittle" — Scooby can talk to other animals and even get them to help him catch monsters.

- Scooby dreams of hamburgers, ice cream cones, and bones.

- A champion among canines — Scooby was awarded the Worcestershire Sauce Medal at the World Games. Go, Scooby!

Tail-Wagging Trivia

Scooby practices karate. (He has to practice, because he's not very good!)

CHAPTER 2:
LIKE, A DUDE NAMED Shaggy!

ZOINKS! SOME SURPRISING SHAGGY SECRETS

- You should *never* take one of Shaggy's shortcuts home. You'll probably end up in a swamp!

- Shaggy once took a security guard job at a Chinese food factory. He figured he would eat while he worked. Now, that's using the old noodle!

- Shaggy has attended over 47 luaus in Hawaii (and stuffed himself at every one)!

- Shaggy's real name is Norville Rogers.

- His phone number is 1-800-LIKE-WOW.

- Shaggy's favorite pastime is eating food. Lots and lots of food — yet he's as skinny as a Slim Jim!

- Shaggy says he never had a lesson in hang gliding, even though he's very good at flying. He just wings it!

- He's known as the "swingingest" gymnast at school!

- Shaggy can spin a pizza on his finger like a basketball (if he can keep it away from his mouth long enough)!

SHAGGY SOUND BITE:
Shaggy has been known to put fish food on a sandwich!
(Ick!)

D-DID S-S-SOMEBODY SAY (GULP) GHOST?!

- Shaggy always carries a copy of *The Cowards' Handbook*.

- In his back pocket, he keeps a pair of scissors. That way, if a ghost grabs him by the shirt, he can quickly snip himself free!

- Shaggy's abandon-ship cry: "Cowards and canines first!"

- He may *pass out* if he meets a hideous ghoul. That is, if he finds the monster *faintly* familiar!

- Shaggy has been known to strap on a pair of roller skates to get away from ghosts faster.

- Shaggy is on his school's track team. No one can beat his time in the 100-monster dash.

From Shaggy's copy of *The Cowards' Handbook*: "In case of bear attack, run as fast as you can!" (Well, duh!)

WHICH VILLAIN SCARED THE WITS OUT OF SHAGGY AND SCOOBY?

A) The Ghost Clown

B) Redbeard the Pirate

C) The Singing Vampire

D) The Green Ghost

(See page 73 for the answer!)

SHAGGY SOUND BITE:
Shaggy says he doesn't
like surprises —
especially spooky ones.
"Ree reither!" adds
Scooby.

MORE GROOVY STUFF ABOUT SHAGGY!

- Shaggy can deal luncheon meat like playing cards. He can even shuffle slices of bread!

- He says he would rather face a ghost than starve to death.

- When the judge says, "Order in the court!" Shaggy answers, "Fifty chili-cheeseburgers to go!"

- Shaggy can open his mouth as big as any-sized sandwich he makes.

- Shaggy has a portable lunch table with collapsible legs, fully stocked with food. It even has a centerpiece with flowers.

- Shaggy says, "If there's one thing worse than a ghost, it's a ghost with muscles!"

- Shag likes to play mad scientist with chemicals.

- An old graveyard is Shaggy's most "un-favorite" place to be, especially at night.

- Shaggy believes that zombies are made of toads and snails and puppy dog tails. (Like, YUCK!)

SHAGGY SOUND BITE:
Shaggy can do a good imitation of a train.
(And a GREAT imitation of a chicken!)

CHAPTER 3:
JINKIES!
The Vibe on Velma!

Very Velma Trivia

What's Velma's trustiest trunk opener in the world? A hairpin!

- Velma's last name is Dinkley.

- She is the shortest and youngest human member of Mystery, Inc. She's also the smartest!

- When Velma gets older, she will become a scientist for NASA. She sets her goals high — sky-high!

"OH, NO! MY GLASSES!"
WHAT HAPPENS WHEN
VELMA LOSES HER SPECS?

- She can't drive a car straight without them.

- She once stopped to talk with a Native American totem pole, thinking it was Shaggy and Scooby.

- During a haunted house case, Velma walked right up to a growling ghost, thinking it was Shaggy with a bad cold.

- One time, Velma threw the wrong switch because she couldn't see. Instead of dropping a net on a monster, she turned out the lights — then everybody was in the dark!

Very Velma Trivia

Shaggy keeps an extra pair of Velma's glasses in his pocket, in case she loses the pair she's wearing. Hopefully they won't get broken when he's running away from zombies!

A GUIDE TO VELMA-SPEAK

- Velma: "Studies show that carnival rides relieve tension." Translation: "Let's go have fun on the roller coaster!"

- Velma: "Oh, I'd love to probe the scientific intricacies of the feat of legerdemain." Translation: "I'd love to learn how to do magic tricks."

- Velma: "Actually, thinking you've seen some place before that you've never been in is quite a common psychological phenomenon." Translation: "You're experiencing déjà vu."

- Velma: "The non-material embodiment or essence or organism that's seen as a specter, wraith, or apparition has been scientifically proven to be sheer myth." Translation: "There's no such thing as a ghost!"

WHICH OF THE FOLLOWING WAS *NOT* A DISGUISED ENTRANCE TO A VILLAIN'S SECRET PASSAGEWAY?

A) A Chinese dragon statue

B) A "Hang in there, baby!" cat poster

C) A mummy's casket

D) An iron maiden

E) A harp case

F) A wine cask

(See page 73 for the answer!)

Very Velma Trivia

Velma tells us
that being a mummy
is about as old as you
can get!

WARNING!

Velma says:
Enter creepy carnivals
at your own risk!

CREEPY CARNIVAL TRIVIA:

- Scooby doesn't like carnival rides like the Ferris wheel and the roller coaster, but he's head-over-paws for the food!

- Attractions at a creepy carnival: The Hall of Horrors, The Dog-Faced Man, Fun House of Mirrors, The Human Fish, and Blog the Magnificent Ferret (10 feet tall!)

- Shaggy's carnival craving: a double order of everything, with a triple order of everything on everything!

CHAPTER 4:
Fred Jones,
LEADER OF
MYSTERY, INC.

- Fred lives at 123 Tuna Lane, Coolsville.

- He can throw a rope lasso like an expert cowboy.

- After a busy day of solving mysteries, Fred will read a book in bed to relax and take his mind off his problems.

FREDDY FACTOID: Fred's favorite thing to say is, "Well, gang, I guess that wraps up another mystery!"

FRED OUTSMARTS VILLAINS WITH BRILLIANT BRAINSTORMS, LIKE . . .

- Get a monster to chase Scooby past a tree where Fred has bent back a big tree branch. When the villain runs past, let the tree branch loose. It smacks the monster into a cart, which rolls down a hill and into a waiting armored car where he'll be locked up tight.

- Trick a villain into chasing Scooby in a haunted wax museum. When the bad guy passes under the hot wax dispenser, let him have it! The hardening wax will hold him tight.

- When a ghoul comes into the room, turn on a high-powered fan that causes him to slide on liquid soap poured on the floor. The creepy villain slides right into a washing machine and the door is slammed shut. And who's the perfect bait for the ghost? Why, it's Scooby-Doo, of course! Better get **LOTS** of Scooby Snacks ready!

HEADS UP, GANG! MORE TRAPS DESIGNED BY FEARLESS FRED:

- Scooby-Doo will lure a ghost up one ramp of a circus train car and run out the other side. When the ghost is in the middle, close both doors.

- Trick a villain with a phony Scooby head. To make one: wrap a bandage around a thick board until it forms a ball for the skull, attach a cantaloupe with a smile cut into it for a snout, and an olive for the nose with toothpicks, add two carrots for ears, and two buttons for eyes.

- Take a toy train and attach two Roman candles to it. Cover it with a Chinese gong. When the villain steps on the gong, Fred will hear it and pull a string attached to a mousetrap. Tied to the mousetrap is a match. The mousetrap is snapped and the match ignites on some sandpaper nearby, lighting the fuses to the Roman candles. The rockets propel the train down some tracks, with the gong and the villain on top of it — right into a waiting cage!

Fred says . . .

- A ghost can't be nobody. It has to be the ghost of somebody.

- A bag of stolen loot is a valuable clue. (No kidding!)

- There are different kinds of ghosts. Some can go through walls and some have to use the door.

- Most people get nightmares after eating too much. (Watch out, Shag and Scoob!)

FREDDY FACTOID: When Fred gets older, he will become a mystery writer. They say you should write about what you know!

WHAT DOES FRED PACK IN THE BACK OF THE MYSTERY MACHINE?

A MYSTERY MACHINE CHECKLIST:

- a built-in radar tracking device
- Daphne's photo darkroom
- ropes
- saw
- mallets
- beach blanket
- a jack
- video monitors
- a BIG supply of Scooby Snacks!
- Shaggy's scooter system
- ladder
- lantern
- clamps
- water jug
- first-aid kit
- computer

MYSTERY MACHINE MOOLA: Daphne's multimillionaire father bought the Mystery Machine for the gang.

WHAT DOES SCOOBY SAY HE'D BUY IF HE HAD $500,000?

A) A diamond-studded muzzle for his cousin Scrappy-Doo

B) The Leaning Tower of Pizza

C) One million hamburgers

D) Stock in the company that makes Scooby Snacks

E) An ultra-high-tech ghost alarm

(See page 73 for the answer!)

Tail-Wagging Trivia

Scooby-Doo once inherited a fortune — in worthless Confederate money!

Tail-Wagging Trivia

Scooby is a terrific cook, but nobody knows it. He always eats his culinary creations before anyone else has a chance to sneak a bite!

SOME SCOOB-PENDOUS RECIPES!

- A Scooby Scoop: a cone with ice cream piled two feet high!

- A Scooby Dog: a hot dog topped with mustard, relish, and Worcestershire sauce.

- Shaggy's Sandwich-Making Song:

> *"The ham slice is connected to the rye bread,*
> *The lettuce is connected to the boiled egg,*
> *The mustard is slapped on a salami slice,*
> *And the cheese is connected to the deviled ham!"*

- Daphne's recipe for a Shaggy Snack:

Mini-pizza with anchovies, pepperoni, and pineapple, topped with a chocolate-dipped cherry.

IS DAPHNE REALLY "DANGER PRONE"? YOU DECIDE. . . .

- During one adventure, while exploring a castle on her own, Daphne got locked in the dungeon.

- She also got trapped on the wrong side of the same castle's drawbridge. Talk about a danger-prone damsel!

- Once Daphne slipped down a hill — right into a zombie!

- She can find trouble just sitting still. Once she sat on a stone bench and it disappeared through a sliding panel in the floor — with Daphne still on it!

- Picture-perfect Daphne even fell into a trap at a carnival photo booth!

DARING DAPHNE TRIVIA:
Daphne is a photographer. She always carries a camera for emergencies (as if she's ever NOT in an emergency)!

FOR DAPHNE, THERE'S NOTHING MORE SERIOUS THAN A FASHION EMERGENCY!

- Most people don't like fog because it's creepy — Daphne doesn't like fog because of the frizz factor.

- When the ghost of Redbeard asked her how walking the plank sounds, Daphne replied, "Corny! I mean, it just isn't done in this day and age!"

- Once Daphne made the ultimate sacrifice — she disguised herself as an old woman in a worn robe with curlers in her hair!

DARING DAPHNE TRIVIA:

When Daphne insisted on getting her picture taken, Fred said: "Sometimes I think Daphne is daffy! This is a ghost hunt, not a beauty contest."

DAPHNE CAN'T DO ONE OF THE FOLLOWING ACTIVITIES. WHICH ONE IS IT?

A) Ride a bicycle

B) Pilot an airplane

C) Develop photographs

D) Write articles for detective magazines

E) Groove with the latest dances

(See page 73 for the answer!)

CHAPTER 6:
WHOO-HOO!
BRING ON THE
Bad Guys!

BRRRR! SOME OF THE CREEPY THINGS YOU FIND WHEN YOU CHASE GHOSTS FOR A LIVING!

MONSTER TRIVIA:

Shaggy guessed the Ghost of Redbeard's secret password: "Yum yum yum, and liverwurst à la mode!"

- The recipe for homemade Ghost Pirate Stew: Bring seawater to a boil and add chains, cobwebs, soap, and ashes from the stove. Serve hot to ghost pirates.

- Books in a haunted library: *Dracula's Manual, Vipers, Bats, Ogres, 101 Ghosts and Ghouls, Everything You Ever Wanted to Know About Witchcraft and Were Afraid to Ask, Spooky Spells,* and *The History of Makeup.*

- Things in the frightening fridge of a mad scientist's lab: Pickled Vampire Wings, Werewolf Snacks, and New, Improved Fried Moonbeams.

THE HYPNOTIC SPELLS OF
THE GHOST CLOWN!

- The Ghost Clown hypnotizes Scooby:

  *"Watch the pretty coin of gold,
  and you will do what you are told.
  You are brave and that's a fact,
  You will do the high-wire act!"*

- The Ghost Clown hypnotizes
  Daphne:

  *"You will pay attention for a time,
  And soon your thoughts will all
  be mine!"*

- The Ghost Clown hypnotizes Shaggy:

  *"You are brave and that's a fact,
  You will do the lion tamer's act!"*

- The Ghost Clown hypnotizes himself when Shaggy
  and Scooby hold up a mirror:

  *"You both have fur, you both are limp,
  You swing through trees like
  a happy chimp!
  Watch the pretty
  coin of gold,
  Be chimpanzees as
  you are told!"*

MONSTER TRIVIA:

The going rate for baiting the Ghost Clown into a trap is one super-duper hero sandwich. With a nasty ghoul like this, Scooby Snacks just aren't enough!

THE OLD GYPSY IS WHO?
THE PHANTOM SHADOW IS WHAT?
AND WHICH WITCH IS WHICH?

- Velma thinks gypsy fortune-telling is nonsense.

- The Phantom Shadow's ominous message on a spooky isle:

  "The first is gone, the rest will go, unless you leave the island and row! Row! Row!"

MONSTER TRIVIA:

Gypsy crystal ball chant:

"Spirits rise and spirits fall, reveal secrets, tell us all!"

- What Velma, disguised as a witch, said to another witch: "I'm a witch like you. What did you expect? A ghost from the coast? A spirit from Spokane? A zombie from Bombay?"

- A witch tells the gang she's going to turn them into lizard and frog stew. But first she'll have to turn them into lizards and frogs!

- Shaggy tries to frighten a witch with a spell of his own:

  "Wicked demons of mist and fog,
  turn this witch into a frog!"

MONSTER TRIVIA: When Scooby and Shaggy hide behind objects like trees, fire hydrants, and people, they can twist their bodies to take on the objects' shapes! Some people can do anything when they're scared!

The Creeper

NAME THAT BAD GUY

The Witch Doctor

Frankenstein's Monster

The Funland Robot

Count Dracula

VILLAINS SAY THE DARNDEST THINGS:

- "You blasted kids! Why don't you mind your own business?"

- "Yes, and I would have gotten away with it, too, if it weren't for those blasted kids and their dog."

- "You kids started snooping around and ruined it for me. Well, you'll pay for that!"

- "A perfect swindle ruined by you meddling kids!"

- "I was going to find the secret recipe and open my own chicken stands, but these durn kids came along and threw a monkey wrench into my plans!"

- "I wanted to frighten off visitors to the castle so I could take over, and I would have, too, if it weren't for you brats!"

- "I swore I'd get even and I would have if it hadn't been for those nosy kids and that dog!"

- "You kids think you're pretty smart! I would have gotten away with it all, too, if you and that dog hadn't come along!"

- "And we'd-a got away if it weren't fer that pesky pair in the cow costume!"

CHAPTER 7: IT'S ALL RELATIVE!

THE MEMBERS OF MYSTERY, INC. HAVE A LOT OF AUNTS, UNCLES, AND COUSINS!

- Velma has an uncle who is an electronics genius.
- Shaggy's uncle Beauregard was a plantation owner and a Civil War general.
- John Maxwell, Daphne's uncle, is a famous movie director.
- Fred's uncle is a colonel in the Air Force and a big shot at the National Space Agency.
- Velma's aunt Thelma is head of the Marine Institute.
- And yet another of Velma's relatives, Uncle Dave Walton, is a U.S. border guard at the Canadian border.
- Daphne has an uncle Matt. He's a cattle rancher.

Tail-Wagging Trivia

Scooby's cousin Yabba-Doo
lives out west on a ranch
and outwits rustlers and
other evildoers just like
a real cowboy!

WHEN THE MYSTERY, INC. GANG WANTS TO ENTERTAIN THEIR RELATIVES, THEY TAKE THEM TO THE LOCAL MALT SHOP. WHICH ONE OF THE FOLLOWING TREATS IS NOT ON THE MENU?

A) Mango Shakes

B) Jumbo Banana Splits

C) Orange Floats

D) Eggplant Surprise Sherbet

E) Chocolate Sundaes with pickles on top

(See page 73 for the answer!)

Tail-Wagging Trivia

Scooby-Doo knows a magic trick: He can make Shaggy's ice cream disappear!

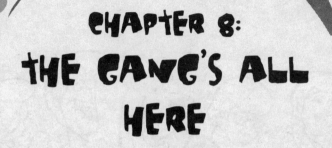

CHAPTER 8:
THE GANG'S ALL HERE

FAST FACTS ABOUT THE GROOVY GANG!

- Shaggy and Scooby-Doo invented a new dance called "The Taffy Twist." It uses real taffy!

- Advice from Shaggy: "Never drop in on a witch uninvited — you know how mad they get!"

- Velma and Shaggy can throw their voices.

- If Scooby hears something when he is asleep, his ear will tap him until he wakes up!

- Velma and Fred always seem to solve the mystery first.

- Shaggy pretends to be an early-American historical figure: "Give me liberty, or give me pizza pie!"

- When Shaggy's got a cold, Velma carries his medicine with her so he doesn't forget to take it.

- Velma can read Chinese.

- Shaggy's groovy things to do on vacation:

  swimming and eating

  tennis and eating

  riding and eating

  eating

- Daphne can fly a helicopter.

- When Velma was young, she learned to read pictographs — Native American picture writings.

- Shaggy's shipboard cry: "All hands on food!"

THEN AGAIN, NOBODY'S PERFECT!

- Shaggy can't read a map. He holds them upside down and gets the gang lost!

- Scooby is not above snatching cheese from a mousetrap.

- Velma says unnecessary things to Shaggy like, "Now be careful!"

- Scoob talks in his sleep when he has doggie nightmares!

- Fred's traps hardly ever work and it's usually Scooby's fault.

- Sometimes Daphne worries more about her hair getting wet than the fact that she's in danger.

- Scooby pretends to be hard of hearing or fakes a sprained ankle to get out of guard duty.

- If Scoob kisses a frog, *it* says yuck.

- The gang will wear their clothes and shoes to bed if they're staying overnight in a haunted house.

- "Canned chicken" — that's what Velma calls Shaggy and Scooby when they hide in a pair of lockers.

- When he's driving, Shaggy gets lost because a fork in the road reminds him of food!

TWO BEST BUDDIES — SHAGGY AND SCOOBY DOO!

- Scooby can blow a whistle and Shaggy can play the bugle. But who needs whistles and bugles when you can yell as loud as they can?

- Shaggy and Scooby would rather have *a steak in them* than go on a *stake out*!

- They can do super imitations of the villains who are after them.

- The Mystery Machine has a lookout hole in the roof for Shag and Scoob to stick their heads through. They say they're looking for ghouls, but they're probably sniffing for hot dogs and hamburgers!

TRIVIA ALERT:

The only thing Scooby-Doo and Shaggy like more than food is each other!

- The movie Shaggy and Scooby always try to catch on the early late show is *I Was a Teenage Blob*.

- If Scooby sees the same ghost twice, Shaggy says he has "déjà BOO!"

- Don't tell anyone: Shag and Scoob wear nightcaps to bed!

- When they're in Chinatown, Scooby and Shaggy always order a Chop Suey Malt.

- Scooby can't whistle a tune. Shaggy's worse.

- Whenever Shaggy plays his guitar, Scooby accompanies him on the drums!

- Once Shag and Scoob flew high into the sky, caught on some helium balloons. Scooby thought they were falling *up*!

WHEN IS SCOOBY NOT AFRAID?

A) When he spots a spider

B) When he surprises a mummy

C) When he's high up in the air

D) When he's alone on guard duty

E) When his friends are in trouble

(See page 73 for the answer!)

CHAPTER 9:
ALL SCOOBY
ALL THE TIME
The Episode
Guide

THE EARLY YEARS:

SCOOBY-DOO, WHERE ARE YOU! 1969–1970
WHAT A NIGHT FOR A KNIGHT

This was the very first episode of Scooby-Doo, what is known in television terms as the series "pilot." The Mystery, Inc. gang encounters a spooky black knight as they try to find a missing archaeologist in a museum.

HASSLE IN THE CASTLE

After seafaring, Shaggy and Scooby run into a mystery ship, where clues from the missing crew lead the gang to a weird island. Once there, they race a phantom to find hidden pirate treasure.

A CLUE FOR SCOOBY-DOO

Another mystery on the high seas — or, in this case, under it! While surfing, Scooby is confronted by the seaweed-covered ghost of a sea captain. The encounter leads our heroes to a scuba adventure in a sunken ship.

MINE YOUR OWN BUSINESS

After spending a stormy night in a western ghost town, the gang is swept up in a mystery involving the spirit of a 150-year-old miner. Hot on the miner's tracks, they soon find themselves in a haunted, abandoned mine.

DECOY FOR A DOGNAPPER

After a prizewinning pooch is stolen, Scooby goes undercover to try and catch the ring of dognappers. Scooby-Doo is nabbed, too, and Fred, Daphne, Velma, and Shaggy track the thieves to a deserted village.

WHAT THE HEX IS GOING ON?

A friend of Daphne's invites the gang to her estate for a visit, but then the friend's uncle suddenly ages 30 years and disappears. Our heroes have a mystery to solve, leading them to the house of a neighbor — a creepy swami.

NEVER APE AN APE MAN

The gang visits Daphne's uncle Max, a movie director, on the set of his newest film. But the production has been halted because a giant ape has been frightening everyone away. It's up to Mystery, Inc. to save the day!

FOUL PLAY IN FUNLAND

Scooby and company investigate a strange seaside amusement park that seems to be running by itself, with no people on the rides. When they go inside, they find a wild robot on the loose, running the whole show!

THE RAGE BACKSTAGE

Shaggy and Scooby find a violin case full of money. While Shaggy goes to find the rest of the gang, a puppet dog distracts Scooby and the money is taken. Clues lead our heroes to a mysterious puppet theater and a ring of counterfeiters.

BEDLAM IN THE BIGTOP

Everyone is quitting the local circus, saying it is jinxed. Even the strongman is afraid to stay. When Scooby and his pals look into the matter, they are met by a ghoulish clown with the power to hypnotize them!

A GAGGLE OF GALLOP-ING GHOSTS

The gang visits a Transylvanian castle, despite the warnings of a scary gypsy who says the place is cursed. They soon learn how true the curse is — they run into Dracula, Frankenstein's Monster, and the Wolf Man when they get there!

SCOOBY-DOO AND A MUMMY, TOO

The members of Mystery, Inc. get trapped on an old cargo plane that takes them to Egypt. Soon they find themselves in an adventure involving a pyramid, a cryptic scroll, gold coins — and a mummy who's after them!

WHICH WITCH IS WHICH

In a dark, gloomy swamp, an armored car full of money has been missing. The gang finds it, but then has to deal with a voodoo-practicing witch and her loyal zombie servant.

SPOOKY SPACE KOOK

Scoob is out there! Our heroes stumble onto what appears to be an abandoned airfield where strange goings-on take place, including bizarre flying objects and glowing otherworldly tracks!

GO AWAY GHOST SHIP

When the 300-year-old ghost of Redbeard the pirate and his ghost crew attack a freighter on a foggy night, Scooby and his super-sleuthing buddies go after the specter. But their boat is cut in two by the pirate's ship and soon they find themselves aboard the ship and face-to-face with the ghostly pirate.

A NIGHT OF FRIGHT IS NO DELIGHT

A millionaire leaves Scooby a fortune in his will. But to get it, Scooby and his pals must spend the night in a haunted castle on a deserted island.

THAT'S SNOW GHOST

While trying to get away for a relaxing ski vacation, our heroes run into another mystery. This one involves the abominable snow creature known as the Yeti and a hidden Tibetan temple.

NOWHERE TO HYDE

Scooby and the gang are trying to trap a jewel thief when they run into the infamous inventor Dr. Jekyll — and then they meet someone they'd rather not: Dr. Jekyll's alter ego, the monstrous Mr. Hyde!

MYSTERY MASK MIX-UP

Daphne gets everyone in trouble when she mistakenly buys a cursed mask in an antique shop. Soon the gang is matching wits with the spirit of an ancient Chinese warlord!

JEEPERS, IT'S THE CREEPER

The gang revives an unconscious bank guard who warns them to "Beware the flame that calls the Creeper." They soon learn just what the guard meant when they accidentally call forth the Creeper while chasing a bank robber.

SCOOBY'S NIGHT WITH A FROZEN FRIGHT

A caveman is found frozen in a block of ice when Shaggy and Scooby go fishing. The Mystery, Inc. gang takes the prehistoric phenomenon to the scientists at Oceanland, but the ice melts and the caveman soon escapes.

THE HAUNTED HOUSE HANG-UP

On their way to a rock concert, the kids are stranded when the Mystery Machine overheats. Searching for water, they enter a gloomy southern mansion. Before long, they encounter a headless body, a floating candle, a moving wooden dummy's head, and other horrors.

A TIKI SCARE IS NO FAIR

While the gang vacations in Hawaii, a ghoulish witch doctor threatens Shaggy and Scooby, warning them of Mano Tiki Tia, a powerful legendary island god come to life.

WHO'S AFRAID OF THE BIG, BAD WEREWOLF?

Shaggy and Scooby are, that's who! The Mystery, Inc. kids follow some curious clues they find while camping in the Pacific Northwest. Their trail leads them through a frightening graveyard and to the empty tomb of a man said to be half man and half wolf!

DON'T FOOL WITH A PHANTOM

A glowing phantom made of wax invades a TV teen dance show while Scooby and his friends are there. When the phantom departs the station manager and the safe are missing. All the clues lead to a spooky wax museum.

THE LEGEND CONTINUES:
THE NEW SCOOBY-DOO MOVIES 1972–1974

GHASTLY, GHOSTLY TOWN
Guest-starring the **Three Stooges**. Mystery, Inc. helps solve a puzzle involving a giant bat and a ghost town in the desert.

THE DYNAMIC SCOOBY-DOO AFFAIR
Guest-starring **Batman and Robin**. The gang helps the Dynamic Duo match wits with the Penguin and the Joker.

SCOOBY-DOO MEETS THE ADDAMS FAMILY
Ghastly goings-on greet Scooby and company when they volunteer to house-sit the **Addams Family's** haunted mansion.

THE FRICKERT FRACAS
Guest-starring comedian **Jonathan Winters**. The gang and Mr. Winters help Maud Frickert solve a mystery involving a ghastly scarecrow, a giant chicken, and a secret formula.

GUESS WHO'S KNOTT COMING TO DINNER!
Guest-starring **Don Knotts** of **Three's Company** fame and **Pleasantville**. Our heroes encounter super-detective and master of disguise Don Knotts when they stop by Moody Manor to ask for directions.

A GOOD MEDIUM IS RARE

Guest-starring comedian **Phyllis Diller**. Scooby-Doo and his friends are locked into an out-of-this-world adventure when they enter the Magic Mansion of Madam Zokar.

SANDY DUNCAN'S JEKYLL AND HYDES

At an old movie studio that is about to be torn down, the gang helps actress **Sandy Duncan** find out who has been disrupting her latest film. Villains include Mr. Hyde, a giant ape, and a Native American.

THE SECRET OF SHARK ISLAND

Guest-starring **Sonny and Cher**. The pop-music duo joins the gang for a horrific night in a run-down resort by the beach. The monster is a giant shark that can walk on land!

THE SPOOKY FOG

Don Knotts guest stars again. Strange things start happening when Officer Don Knotts invites the gang to spend the night in the local jail.

SCOOBY-DOO MEETS LAUREL AND HARDY

Snowbound high jinks abound when the gang crosses paths with comic duo **Laurel and Hardy** at a ski lodge in Vermont. They join forces to track Bigfoot.

THE GHOST OF THE RED BARON

Once more Mystery, Inc. teams up with the **Three Stooges**. This time, they hunt for the ghost of a WWI flying ace.

THE GHOSTLY CREEP FROM THE DEEP

Guest-starring the **Harlem Globetrotters** basketball team. Everyone bands together to double-team the ghosts of the legendary pirate Redbeard and his crew.

THE HAUNTED HORSEMAN OF HAGGLETHORN HALL

Guest-starring singer/actor **Davy Jones of The Monkees.** Our heroes help Davy solve the mystery of an ancient haunted fortress in Scotland and the fearsome phantom knight who dwells there.

THE PHANTOM OF THE COUNTRY MUSIC HALL

It's Southern-fried horror as the kids help country singer/actor **Jerry Reed** capture a creep that's been scaring the Opry-goers.

THE CAPED CRUSADER CAPER
The gang assists the caped crusaders, **Batman and Robin**, as they protect the innocent from the threatening twosome, the Penguin and the Joker.

THE LOCH NESS MESS
Scoob and the gang run into the **Harlem Globetrotters** again as they seek to uncover the mystery of Paul Revere's ghost.

THE MYSTERY OF HAUNTED ISLAND
The **Harlem Globetrotters** help Scooby Doo and the gang outwit some ghastly ghouls who are determined to keep everyone on a haunted island awake.

THE HAUNTED SHOWBOAT
Mystery, Inc. and guest-stars **Josie and the Pussycats** hunt for the 100-year-old ghost of Injun Joe on the Mississippi River.

SCOOBY-DOO MEETS JEANNIE
As in, "I Dream of . . ." The teenage sleuths and **Jeannie** travel back in time to help a prince battle an evil spirit.

THE SPIRITED SPOOKED SPORT SHOW
Guest-star and comedic actor **Tim Conway** plays a coach who enlists Scooby and pals to help him rid a school of ghosts.

THE EXTERMINATOR
The gang needs to "get smart" when they join actor **Don Adams**, in his role as bug exterminator to the stars. Together, they try to rid a haunted house of its varmints.

WEIRD WINDS OF WINONA
Scooby and company get behind the steering wheel of **Speed Buggy** to quiet the midnight winds haunting a small town.

THE HAUNTED CANDY FACTORY
The kids help guest-star **Cass Elliot** from the **Mamas and the Papas** defeat two ghoulish green globs that are trying to take over her candy factory.

SCOOBY-DOO MEETS DICK VAN DYKE
The kids help actor **Dick Van Dyke** expose a group of ghosts who are scaring away customers from his newly purchased carnival.

ANSWERS TO QUESTIONS FROM
VELMA'S TRIVIA FILE:

QUESTION #1 (page 8) WHAT IS SCOOBY-DOO'S REAL NAME?
Answer — C) Scoobert

QUESTION #2 (page 18) WHICH VILLAIN SCARED THE WITS OUT OF SHAGGY AND SCOOBY?
Answer — Trick question. They ALL did!

QUESTION #3 (page 26) WHICH OF THE FOLLOWING WAS *NOT* A DISGUISED ENTRANCE TO A VILLAIN'S SECRET PASSAGEWAY?
Answer — B) A "Hang in there, baby!" cat poster

QUESTION #4 (page 35) WHAT DOES SCOOBY SAY HE'D BUY IF HE HAD $500,000?
Answer — C) One million hamburgers

QUESTION #5 (page 41) DAPHNE CAN'T DO ONE OF THE FOLLOWING ACTIVITIES. WHICH ONE IS IT?
Answer — A) Ride a bicycle

QUESTION #6 (page 52) WHEN THE MYSTERY, INC. GANG WANTS TO ENTERTAIN THEIR RELATIVES THEY TAKE THEM TO THE LOCAL MALT SHOP. WHICH ONE OF THE FOLLOWING TREATS IS NOT ON THE MENU?
Answer — D) Eggplant Surprise Sherbet

QUESTION #7 (page 60) WHEN IS SCOOBY NOT AFRAID?
Answer — E) When his friends are in trouble

Congratulations! Now that you've read this book, you have achieved official super-sleuthing Scooby expert status. Scooby-Doo is proud of you!

ABOUT THE AUTHOR
Jesse Leon McCann, extreme Scooby fan

Jesse Leon McCann has watched just about every Scooby cartoon ever created, and read tons of Scooby books, which pretty much certifies him as a Scoob-erific expert. As a writer, Jesse has worked on Scooby-Doo coloring and activity books, comic books, Scholastic's Scooby-Doo 3-D Mysteries, and even a how to draw Scooby and the gang book.

What has he learned from all this Scooby-intense research? Well, for one thing, he thinks everyone is a little like Scooby-Doo. Sometimes we have to face scary situations, because our friends or family need us to be there. Frequently, we will become very creative when met with a difficult challenge. Often, we laugh at trouble to relieve the tension. And some of us eat too many snacks!

Zoinks! Sometimes Jesse even gets a craving for a . . . Scooby Snack!!